ISBN 0.7119.1952.6   Order No. OP 45582

Exclusive distributors:
BOOK SALES LIMITED,
8/9 Frith Street, London W1V 5TZ, UK.
MUSIC SALES CORPORATION,
225 Park Avenue South, New York, NY 10003, USA.
MUSIC SALES PTY LIMITED,
120 Rothschild Avenue, Rosebery, NSW 2018, Australia.
To the Music Trade only:
MUSIC SALES LIMITED,
8/9 Frith Street, London W1V 5TZ, UK.

All pictures by kind permission of London Features International except as listed below.
© 1989 Seal Rocks Pty Ltd Front Cover, p4 (L), 5 (R), 8, 9 (+inset), 11, 12 (T&B), 14 (L), 15, 16, 17,
18 (T&B), 19, 22, 23, 24, 25, 27 (T&B), 32 (L&BL).
Editorial research by Susan Black
Designed by Peter Dolton
Design and production in association with
Book Production Consultants, 47 Norfolk Street, Cambridge
Picture research by Debbie Dorman
Picture credits: London Features International
Typeset by Cambridge Photosetting Services
Origination by Anglia Graphics, Bedford
Printed in England by Baker Brothers Limited, Pontefract

Omnibus Press
London/New York/Sydney/Cologne

THE JASON DONOVAN STORY

By building a career in show business, Jason Donovan has hardly gone against the grain. The son of actor Terence Donovan and actress Sue McIntosh, fate seems to have played a major part from the word go.

After his parents' divorce when Jason was only five, Jason was brought up by his father, so he witnessed how the life of an actor could be full of ups and downs. "I saw my dad in work and I saw him out of work," Jason now reflects. "There must have been times when it was hard for him, though I guess I didn't appreciate what he was going through. I knew that being an actor wasn't all glamour but, even still, I can't remember really wanting to be anything else."

His dad, on the other hand, wanted Jason to be anything but an actor. "He certainly tried to put me off and although I started getting TV work quite early on, dad insisted that I stay at school, sit all of my exams, and then get a proper job!"

At the age of 11 Jason took on his first television role in the series *Skyways*. This was also Jason's first meeting with Kylie Minogue, who was cast as his sister.

Jason met up with Kylie again on the Neighbours set but when asked, Kylie doesn't seem to have been too impressed by their first meeting. "At that stage you're not all that interested in boys or what they look like," she claims, "so I don't remember Jason too well from that period. I do remember that he was really quite chubby and he had a bit of a bowl haircut."

Jason's first big acting break came in a children's TV series with the memorable title, *I Can Jump Puddles*. He then worked on other TV programmes such as *Home*, *Marshlands*, and *Golden Pennies* and at sixteen there were not many young actors around with experience to match Jason's.

It shouldn't have been a surprise then, when Australia's Channel 7 offered Jason an audition to appear in *Neighbours*. Although his dad was fully aware that Jason could handle a regular role, he again persuaded his son to continue with his studies for a little while longer.

Six months later *Neighbours* had been written off as a commercial flop and sold to a rival station – Channel 10. Once again,

Jason got the chance to audition for the show and, having completed his Higher School Certificate, this time there was nothing to stop him. Immediately successful, Jason found himself cast as the new Scott Robinson, replacing Darius Perkins, and promptly started work on the serial's relaunch in January 1986.

After only one year in *Neighbours* Jason won the coveted Logie award for "Best New Talent". By then, he had set his sights on a move towards a musical career.

He was, however, particularly anxious that the critics shouldn't misjudge his motives. "I've always loved singing as well as acting, so it wasn't completely out of the blue, like some people have said. When I was a kid I was in the Australian Boys Choir and I learned the piano. When my acting career started taking off I just thought it would be good to add another string to my bow – so I started taking singing lessons".

Jason freely admits that the pop career was not an easy step for him to make, however. "Believe it or not, I actually kicked the idea around for a year and a half before plucking up the courage. It's something I've always wanted to do, but I didn't feel that I was ready to do it professionally right then. Still, I laid down a couple of tracks during a break in filming and was later approached by Pete Waterman to do some work with Mike Stock, Mat Aitken and himself.

WAR HERO

With his début single 'Nothing Can Divide Us' shooting to number 5 in the UK charts, Jason undertook yet another project. During a three month break from filming *Neighbours* Jason took on the role of Happy Houston in the TV mini-series *The Heroes*.

It was around this time of course, that Jason had his long golden curls cut back, and many 'journalists' have put this down to the influence of image-makers at PWL, his record company. The facts are far less sinister, however, with Jason having to have his hair cut for his new, 1940s acting role.

"I'd had my hair quite long for ages, so it did take some getting used to," he admits. "But I think I'd even shave my head if the role called for it."

Playing the part of a Second World War army officer engaged in a plot to sink Japanese ships in Singapore Harbour, Jason's role was a far cry from Ramsay Street and he was understandably very pleased with his most challenging acting role to date.

JASON DONOVAN

FULL NAME: Jason Sean Donovan

BORN: 1st June 1968, in Melbourne.

HEIGHT: 5ft 11ins

EYES: Blue

WEIGHT: 10 and a half stone

QUALIFICATIONS:
"I passed my Higher School Certificate in 1985. It's Australia's equivalent to your O levels."

CHILDHOOD HOBBIES:
"I used to pretend I was Superman and jump off large objects, often ending up on top of my friends."

HOME:
"A 1920's style house in Melbourne which my father and I renovated"

HIS GARDEN:
"I'd love to get more time to work on my garden. It has a big walnut tree in it which the local cockatoos love to feed off."

FAVOURITE PASTIME:
"Surfing. I try and get away to the beach as often as I can, as surfing is a great release for me. There is nothing like the feeling of being pushed along by a wave.

FAVOURITE ACTOR:
"I particularly admire Michael J Fox. He has great ability and has done some brilliant movies. I most enjoyed Back To The Future. I also like Michael Douglas and Meryl Streep."

BEST HOLIDAY:
"I went to Maui once. It's an island just off Hawaii. It was the best holiday because I really enjoyed the contrast between the traditional Hawaii and the Hawaii of modern days. There was fantastic surf, great shopping, a warm climate and probably the best hotel I've ever stayed in."

FIRST SCREEN KISS:
"With Charlene, of course, in Neighbours."

RELIGION:
"I don't belong to any religion, but I don't dismiss it either. I attended a Catholic school, but I was never a Catholic"

BODY MAINTENANCE:
"I try to go for a run every morning and I swim in the ocean every chance I get. Other than that I eat mostly healthy foods."

23

24

JASON~ THE QUOTES

"I'd love to go on a holiday in space. Wouldn't everybody?! Experiencing weightlessness would be insane!! The food in tablet form would be hard to get used to, but I reckon I'd do it!"

"I was stung by a jellyfish once while I was swimming. It was just a stinging irritation. It just sticks to your body. Quite frightening really."

"I had a conversation with Pete (Waterman) one day in a car on the way to the Cotswolds to see his collection of cars, and said to him that it would be great to do a cover version, and also that I'd like to do something that was slower because it was such a dance LP. 'Sealed With A Kiss' wasn't my suggestion, it was Pete's. I didn't know the song till I went to a record shop and bought a version of it!"

"My dad actually put out a record in the late seventies. It was a sort of *rocky* number. I can't remember what it was called, ha-ha, but it wasn't a hit or anything."

"People cope with nerves in different ways. Some smoke, others use worry beads – I play with a Russian ring to calm myself down."

"Paul McCartney is my hero – I'd love to meet him. People forget I'm a fan too. I went to the Duran Duran show in Docklands. Paul Young and George Michael were there, and I got butterflies talking to them."

"A lot of people see Kylie and I out together, and they don't understand that we're together because we're friends, and that there's no more to it than that."

"When I was a kid, my dad once got me Muhammed Ali's autograph. I was really knocked out, ha-ha! In fact, I was so afraid of losing it, that I kept it in a little toy safe in my bedroom. And guess what? Yeah, I lost the combination!"

"I always try to stay healthy by eating a lot of fresh food and drinking lots of water. The problem is, when I'm at home, I tend to stock up the fridge with the intention of eating salad all week. But if I'm working late, I'll just grab a take-away instead. So when I open my fridge at the end of the week, it stinks!"

"I've got this policeman's uniform that I used to wear to play in, which is something I've kept from childhood. . . I used to play in it all the time. It's still hanging in my wardrobe."

"I simply adore postcards. I started my collection when I first went overseas, and I've got hundreds now. I try to keep them on display at home, and I put as many as possible up on the wall. The only trouble is they're a nightmare when it comes to dusting!"

"I remember one day I was at home, I spotted this gigantic spider's web at the top of the tree outside my window. So I started to climb it and I crawled into this web, and there was this big, gloomy spider at the end of it. It just looked at me, and then we had this amazing fight where he tried to wrap me up like Spiderman, and then I got a better look at him when the sun streamed through the web, and it turned out that it *was* Spiderman, ha-ha-ha-ha-ha!!!! No, just pulling your leg there. . ."

"I'm starting to get used to the 26 hour plane flight from England to Australia now. I'm usually so tired that I just sleep all the way."

"When I was young I used to stand in front of a mirror with a tennis racket, pretending to be a pop star. . . I think most people do, but they don't really want to admit it."

DISCOGRAPHY

SINGLES

NOTHING CAN DIVIDE US/NOTHING CAN DIVIDE US (Instrumental)
PWL 17
August 1988 (Reached number 5)

ESPECIALLY FOR YOU/ALL I WANNA DO IS MAKE YOU MINE
PWL 24
November 1988 (No 1)

TOO MANY BROKEN HEARTS/WRAP MY ARMS AROUND YOU
PWL 32
February 1989 (No 1)

SEALED WITH A KISS/JUST CALL ME UP
PWL 39
May 1989 (No 1)

ALBUM

TEN GOOD REASONS
HF7
May 1989 (No 1)